minus 25 years 25 projects

25 years, a thousand thanks

our thanks go first and foremost to our passionate team: our designers, technical draughtsmen and furniture makers are all professionals who take incredible pride in what they do. their daily commitment is invaluable. it has been a privilege to work with them: a design is only taken to the next level when these professionals start working with it.

we also want to thank all our clients for the opportunities they have provided us. in particular, we would like to thank our clients from the early days, who placed their trust in us even though we did not have many references at the time. thanks to our clients, we have been able to work in many new and inspiring places, both in belgium and abroad: from poperinge to france, from the coast of sardinia and the beaches of miami to the dome of jean nouvel's doha tower.

even greater is the happiness we feel when our clients trust us to help them shape their home.
finally, we would like to thank the generations that preceded us for the solid foundations.

the essence of living

for the past 25 years, minus has been decoding the essence of living. all this time, founders sophie popelier and wim carton have taken the less-is-more approach, creating pared-down, tranquil living spaces imbued with contemplative stillness, where everything has its place. while their minimalist design language has found many fans outside belgium – as far away as doha and miami – belgium's westhoek region, where they design and produce everything, continues to nurture their creativity. a conversation about creative autonomy, the joys and burdens of a family business, and the role of aesthetics. 'when people come to us for a design, we really take care of everything – from the first line on paper down to the very last screw.'

the vision behind all minus designs is to capture 'the essence of living'. so how do you interpret this?

wim carton: 'i see it as a quest for what you need to feel at home somewhere. it's about striking the perfect balance where nothing is redundant. but where you're not deprived of anything either. coming home is pausing in a world that rarely stops. by eliminating all visual stimuli, we create a physical space where the brain naturally unwinds.'
sophie popelier: 'clutter affects my peace of mind. our living space exudes peace and order – every object has its place, its reason for being. everything we buy or incorporate in this space is there for a reason. we value the aesthetics of omission. for us, 'less is more' is not a cliché but a guiding principle.'

how is this philosophy conveyed in your designs and projects?

wc: 'we think a design is good when all lines that can be erased have been erased. that is when it has been stripped down to its essence. during my studies at sint-lucas, a lecturer showed me constantin brâncuși's stylised bird sculpture: he had omitted all the ballast, leaving just enough to capture the essence of the bird. to me, that's what a good designer should do: keep erasing until you can't. because if you do eliminate something at this stage, there would be nothing left. as a designer, that's where i want to be. you can clearly see this drive for essence in our design language, but also in the spatial organisation of a home.'
sp: 'we are obsessed with lines and proportions. each line must resonate with the greater whole; nothing is left to chance. the entire team shares this sensitivity to detail, from design to installation. there is a shared commitment to aesthetic precision.'

how do you maintain the balance between concept, functionality and aesthetics?

sp: 'we always start from functionality. to create visual calm, we strive to make as many elements as possible invisible or to integrate them. at times, this requires well-thought-out choices. during the design process, we talk to our clients at length to understand how far they are willing to go.'
wc: 'our designs are often conceptual. like our own home in reningelst: a beam-shaped glass pavilion with floating kitchen cabinets. but there can be no concept without beauty or functionality. in everything we make, aesthetics are a basic requirement. a design can only be successful when these three elements are in balance.'

minimalism is often criticised for being cold and feeling like a hospital room. what's your take on this?

sp: 'above all, we want to be timeless. our interiors must still look fresh in twenty years. that's why we love white so much. white never goes out of style. but even in white, there are countless nuances.'
wc: 'designing is a continuous balancing act for us. an interior should tell a story of individuality, but at the same time, it must be neutral enough to instil a sense of tranquillity. our interiors are not showpieces but modest canvases that serve as a space for the life that unfolds in them.'

you always design for your client. how do you manage the tension between your own ideas and the client's expectations?

wc: 'as a designer, i want to be 100% satisfied with what i have created. i will always stay true to our minimalist design language. that's our dna. we are incapable of designing in any other style. we just can't. and the clients who choose to work with us know this.'
sp: 'to create a good design, you need to get to know your clients. we invest a lot of time and energy into this. by talking and seeing how they live, we can design a home that they will want to live in. we are only happy when the clients are happy.'

minus's signature style is very recognisable. how did you develop such a consistent body of work?

wc: 'when we established minus, we were determined to adhere to the minimalist style. thanks to the income generated by our furniture studio, we could afford to be very selective in our choices. we only accepted design commissions where we could really make our mark. and ultimately, this paid off. when clients come to us, it's because they believe in our style.'

how do you build a coherent portfolio without repeating yourself?

sp: 'by starting from a blank slate for every project and continuing to challenge ourselves. we will never copy an old design in a new project. it also helps that there are two creative minds at the helm. in economic terms, it obviously makes sense to do the same thing two or more times, but that's just not how we work.'

you both studied interior architecture at sint-lucas in ghent. which insights from this period do you use to this day?

wc: 'that training shaped me, not just as a designer, but also as a person. the lecturers broadened my views and taught me to think critically. precisely because we were taught subjects like philosophy and psychology, we can now better sense and understand clients.'
sp: 'essentially, it was an art course where you learned to think out of the box.'

wim, you are the seventh generation of a family of joiners. was it a given that you would take over the family business?

wc: 'it was taken for granted from childhood. but i was rebellious, i wasn't interested in making windows and doors. i enrolled at sint-lucas with the goal of becoming a designer. after working for a few years, sophie and i realised that as a designer, you are nothing if you don't have the people it takes to bring your designs to life. when my father wanted to sell the workshop, we decided to take it over on condition that we could turn it into a furniture workshop.'

julien carton adds an extension to the workshop and signs the concrete.

was it always your dream to have your own design studio?

sp: 'my sole ambition has always been to make beautiful things. having a business didn't hold much appeal for me. but when wim and i took over the furniture workshop, the idea was always to combine it with a design studio. we felt that it would allow us to make furniture that no one else could or wanted to make. and we pulled it off. thanks to our craftsmanship and extensive know-how, we have the technical skill to produce almost anything. often, when we draw something, the joiners will say, "it can't be done." in that case, we look for a solution together. that's our strength.'

can you share key turning points in your career?

wc: 'besides the decision to take over the family business, our first participation in interieur kortrijk had a tremendous impact. we presented a very conceptual kitchen, which was an international hit. this led to talks in belgium and abroad, as well as design commissions. our subsequent participations in this design and interior event also always boosted minus's profile.'

how do you work together?

wc: 'sophie and i are each other's polar opposites: i am a methodical person, and sophie is not. this has the advantage that we complement each other perfectly. sophie is much more artistic and still surprises me with ideas i would never come up with. i excel in technical elaboration. in that sense, we work sequentially, rather than together.'

being good at what you do does not mean you are good at business. how do you reconcile the two?

wc: 'we grew organically, starting out with two employees in the workshop. after ten years, we had ten employees. we almost ended up with burnout because we had too much on our plates. we did everything together: design, admin, production preparation, and site supervision. we wore too many hats and worked long, long hours. during our training, we learned how to think and dream, but they didn't teach us about costing and budgeting. so sophie and i took a one-year course at vlerick, specifically for smes.'

did minus change course after this training?

wc: 'after graduating from vlerick, we appointed an advisory board. they said, "you have a great product. we are going to help you grow exponentially." they suggested we accept five 'elite' projects every year. they aimed to utilise all the research and development for these projects to create a more affordable line, enabling us to install twenty kitchens annually. we would only focus on these top-of-the-range projects. but this clashed with our way of working and our client approach. so we deliberately opted not to grow our business further. with a staff of twenty, you can just about maintain the horizontal hierarchy we aspire to. we're control freaks who want to get to know every client and personally check every cabinet that leaves the workshop. growth seems to be the only option in business, but that's not how we see it.'

how does sustainability influence your work?

sp: 'it is implicit in everything we design and produce because we make things that are still valuable after twenty years. timelessness is sustainability.'
wc: 'twenty-five years ago, we were already creating designs that were made to last for more than one generation. this is the essence of sustainability. and we achieve this by using only the best materials and techniques.'

finally, what about the next 25 years? where does the future of minus lie?

sp: 'the future of minus definitely lies in our expertise. thanks to our know-how and skills, we are able to differentiate ourselves from the rest. i think this is also the reason behind our international success.'
wc: 'we are proud of what we have achieved with minus. the road to excellence is hard work and is never-ending. our way of life and living is constantly evolving, and as a design studio, we need to respond to that. we are also seeing that, in contrast to social equality, people are looking for interiors that are unique and bespoke down to the smallest detail. this comprehensive form of customisation is our future.'

the minus headquarters are located in poperinge in a 25-by-25-metre volume next to the workshop. in addition to the company's offices, it also comprises a living space. the design is all about playing with contrast, creating nice visual tension by pairing dark oak parquet and a dark cast floor with pure white walls and cabinets. the kitchen is conceived as a white box within the living area. the floor and worktop in chiselled carrara marble add tactility, while a sleek white wall consisting of five sliding doors conceals all the kitchen functions, with the insides finished in dark-stained zebrawood. the office is designed according to the clean desk principle: everything is locked away behind sliding doors to prioritise calm and focus. there are vistas and sight lines throughout the building, drawing daylight into the spaces and creating ever-changing perspectives.

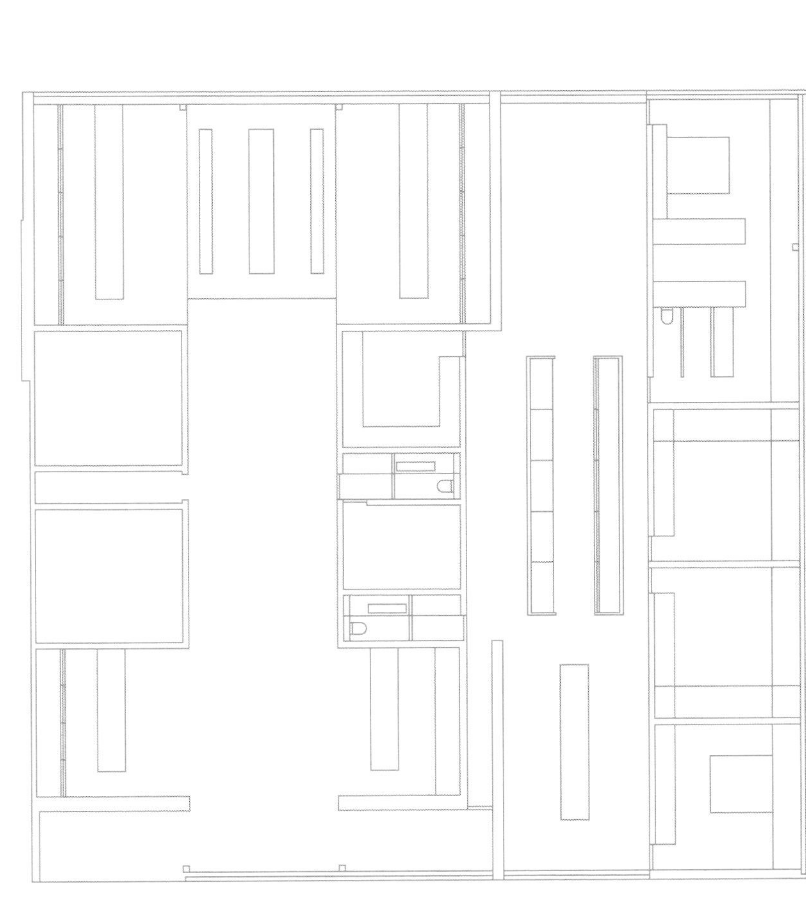

for biennale interieur 08, we designed a square space with a centrally positioned square kitchen island with fronts in brushed and dark-stained oak, finished with a stainless-steel worktop. the three functions are hidden behind a wall with pivoting doors: the pantry and kitchen appliances are on the left, with the wine cellar on the right. originally conceived for a design and interior fair, the kitchen was subsequently repurposed in a castle, where it is still in use today.

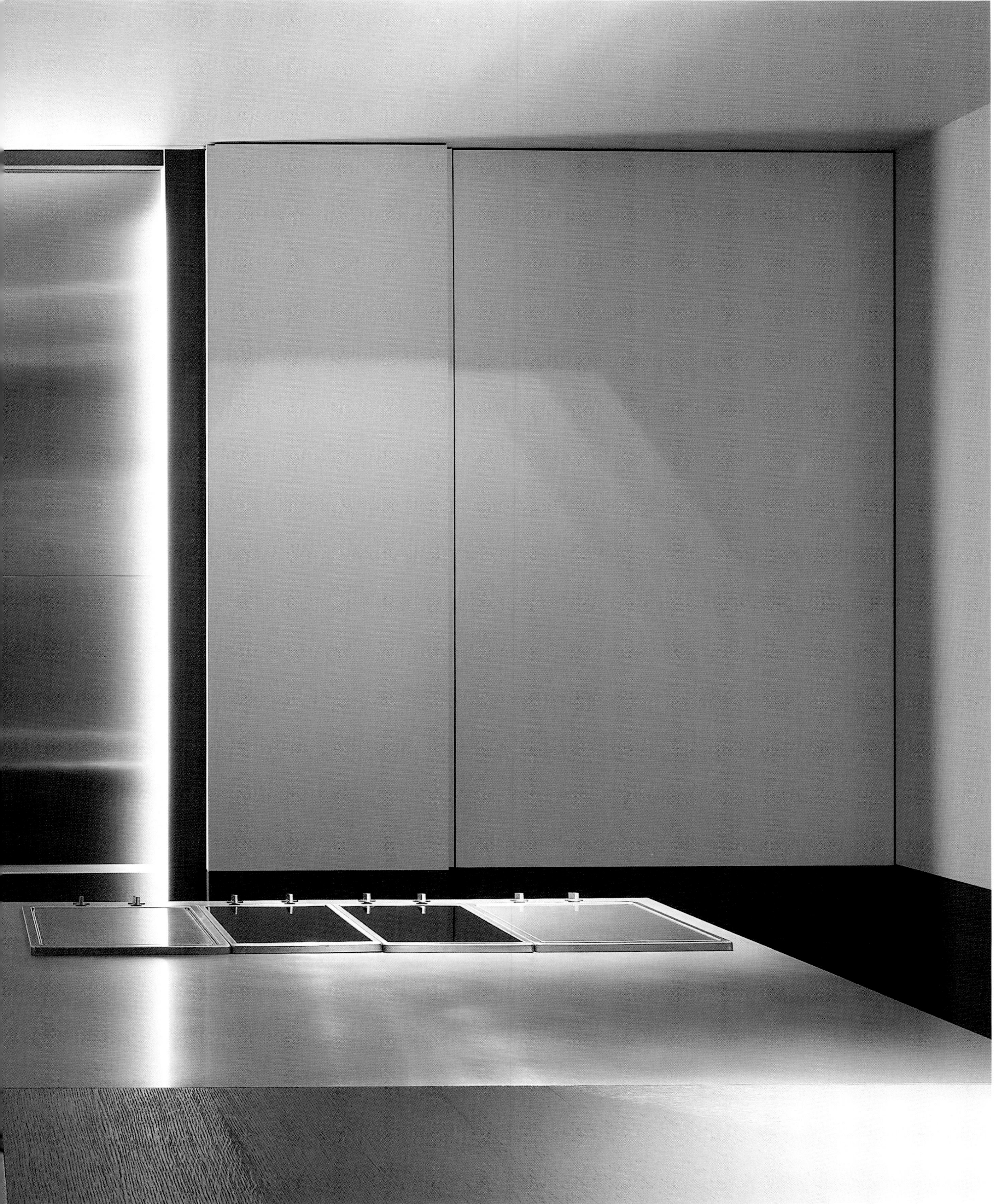

the kitchen design for biennale interieur 2010 starts from two volumes: a white worktop and a long teak wall unit that has been installed perpendicular to it. the envelope of the stand is made entirely from zinc. the floating volume contains the extractor hood and a built-in storage, and can be electrically raised and lowered to the desired height. the wall unit can be fully closed or opened and has a meticulously designed storage area. the lines of the handles extend into the ceiling, where they merge seamlessly into sleek light lines thanks to the integrated lighting.

minus

kreon, which specialises in architectural tools of light, asked us to develop a design concept for its monobrand stores. it was first rolled out in paris, the city of lights. the contrast between light and dark was our starting point. dark-stained parquet, a dark ceiling, and pure white cabinets and walls create visual tension. daylight is filtered through custom-made slats, creating a dimensional light effect. pivoting panels are used to reveal or block the view from the street. the parquet was deliberately laid lengthwise, emphasising the narrowness and depth of the space.

" less is more "

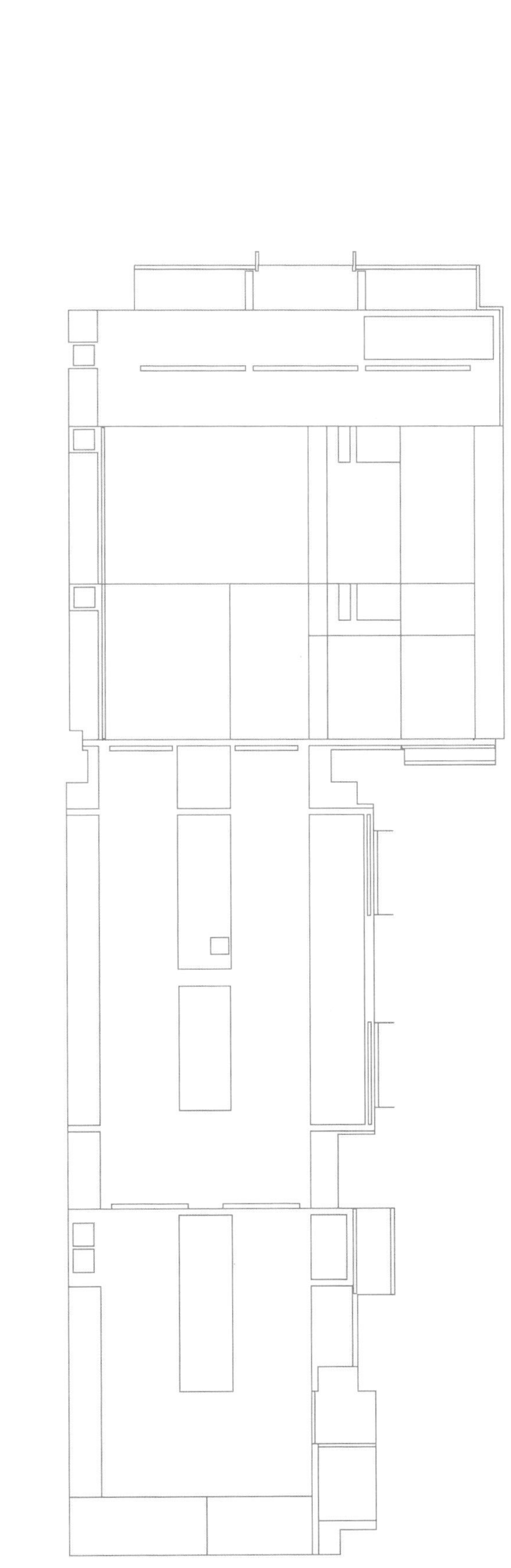

we were approached to design john eskenazi's art gallery in notting hill, london, in collaboration with architect oscar van overeem. the brief was to create a warm, intimate atmosphere. upon entering, the gaze is immediately drawn to anish kapoor's artwork. the walnut flooring and custom cabinetry cast a deep, natural glow, creating a nice contrast with the matt chiselled stone bases. solid walnut was used for the shutters to temper the brightness of the outdoor light. the handleless cabinet doors blend into the space, highlighting the artworks and books and imbuing the space with a sense of tranquillity.

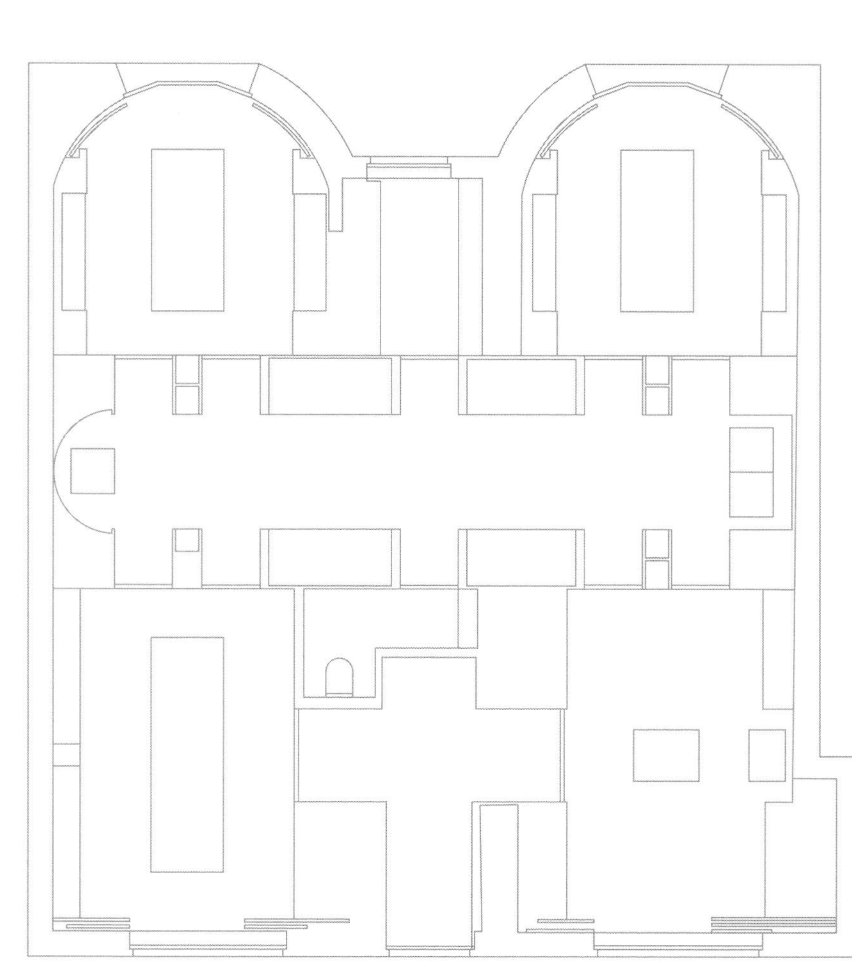

coussée & goris created a concrete extension for an existing house at the belgian seaside. minus was asked to design the kitchen, bedroom and bathroom. the cool grey of the concrete was paired with walnut walls and pivoting panels. we opted for sleek volumes to enhance the solid architectural design.

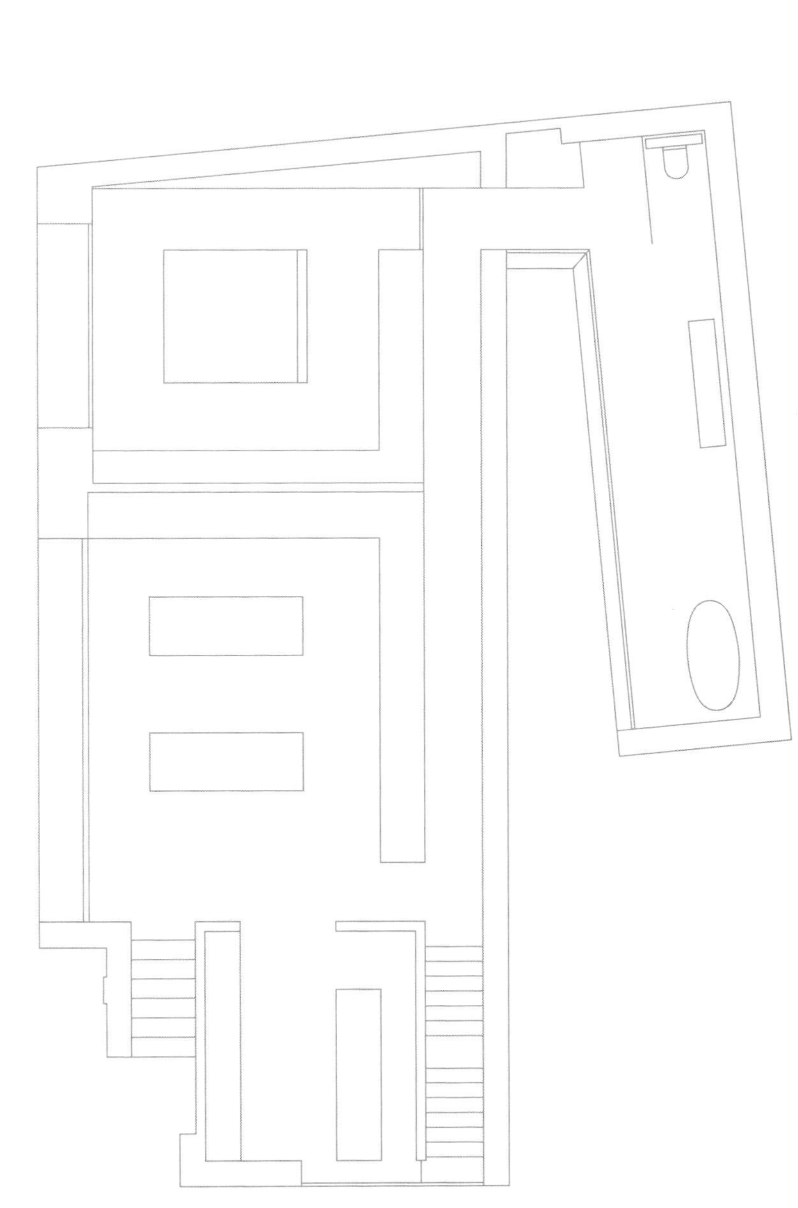

this kitchen was designed for an interior design fair. copper and natural larch add striking accents to the all-white box. the worktop can be fully enclosed with lids that fold down electronically. the insides of the lids are lined with copper and serve as a backsplash. opposite the kitchen sink is a floating volume with a six-metre-long roll-up door. a pivoting door next to the kitchen counter provides access to an integrated desk space. the larchwood floor adds warmth and texture to the sleek design.

minus

minus
minus

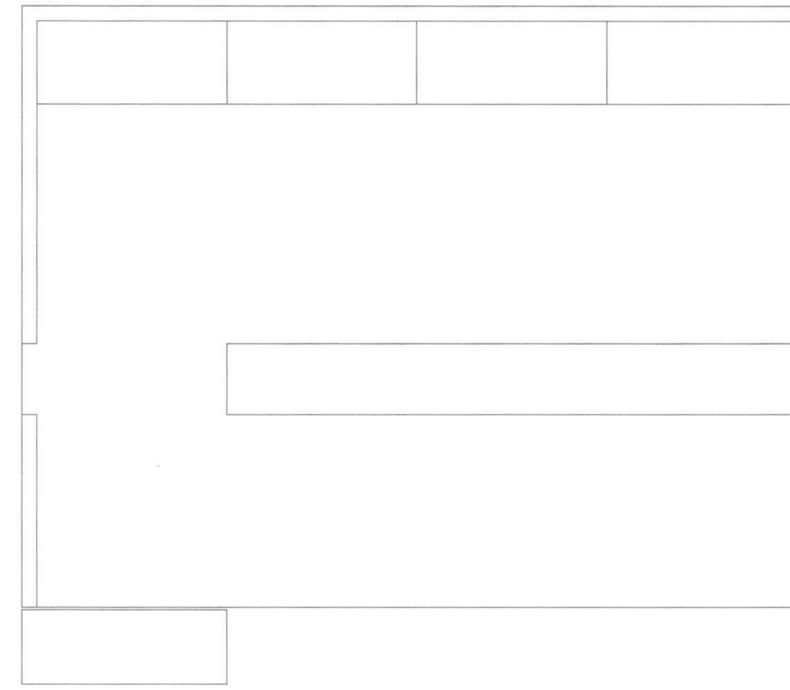

originally, this house was quite dark, with limited natural light. minus was asked to maximise light and brighten the interior as well as create a holiday atmosphere, with views of the pool and beautiful garden from every room. an extension was designed in the style of the existing house. concrete tiles were used indoors and outdoors and served as the reference for all alignments. the kitchen is designed so that all the appliances are discreetly hidden behind lacquered cabinet doors. vistas on either side of the cabinet walls provide a visual connection to the garden.

the exterior architecture of this classic country home contrasts sharply with its sleek, clean interior. the warmth of the natural materials – oak and carrara marble – is enhanced by the clean, white walls. the understated design and materials frame the views of the surrounding countryside.

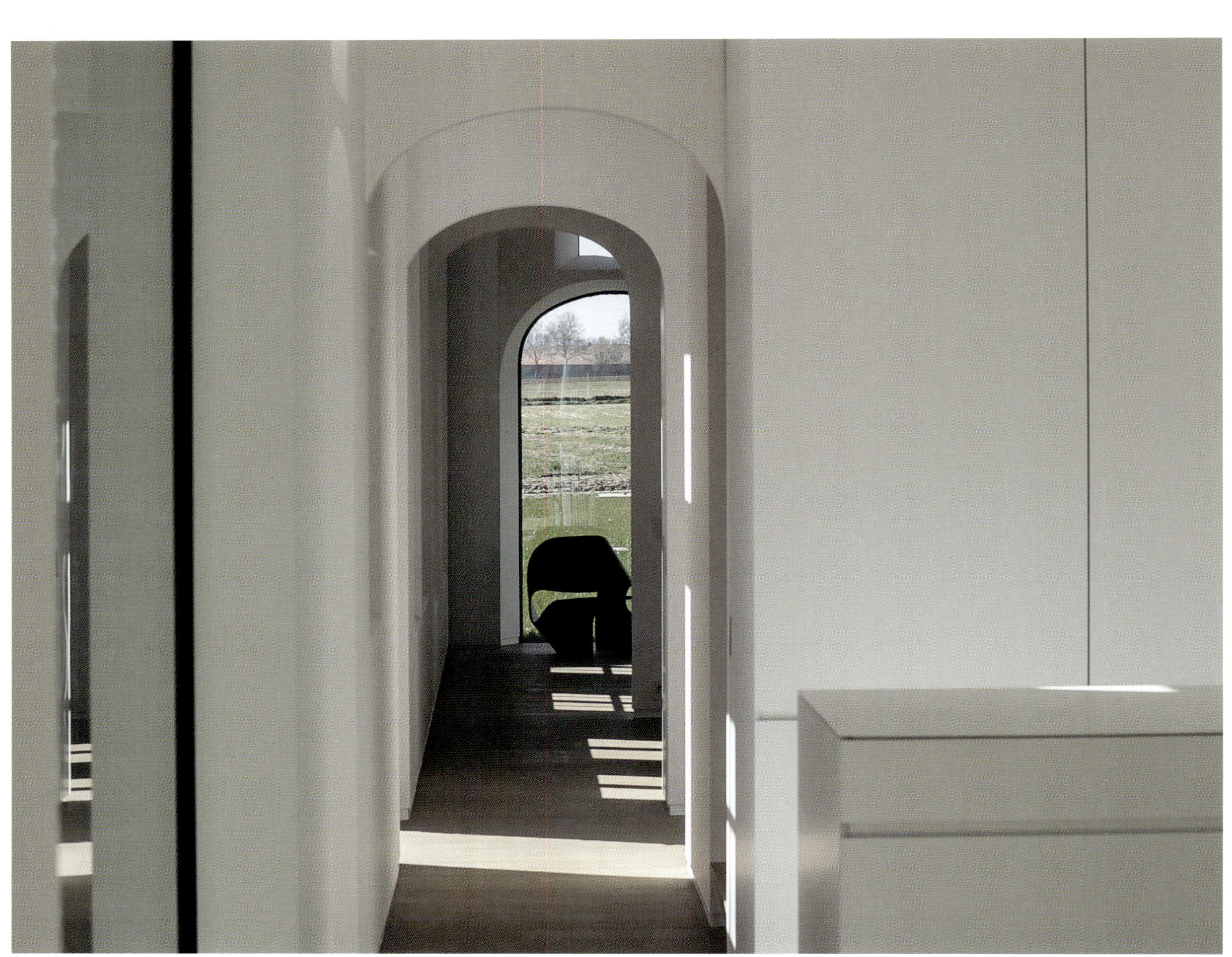

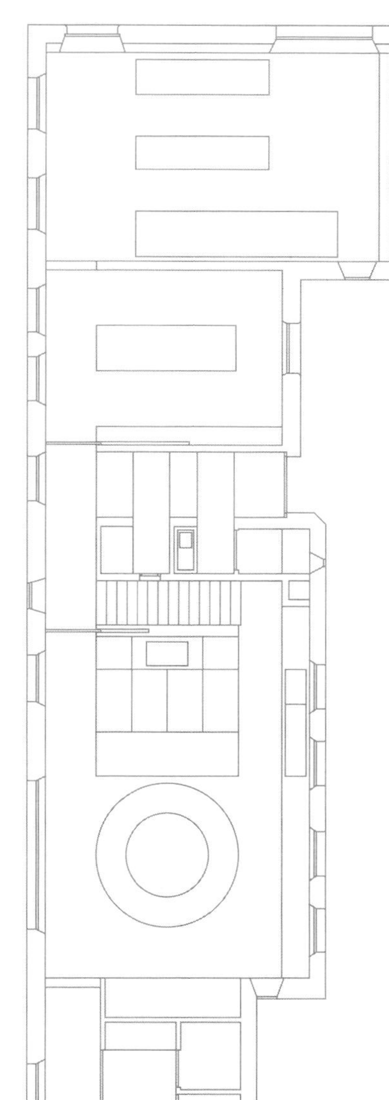

the existing building was extended with a newly designed volume. in the original volume with brick vaulted ceilings, the entranceway and offices were executed in a dark colour palette. the new-build deliberately counterbalances the theatrical aspect of the old volume with materials that contrast sharply with it. the double height of the kitchen ceiling creates a sense of space, which is accentuated by the alignment of the height of the windows and the kitchen cabinets. the altar-like kitchen island serves as a central focal point while cabinets camouflage the kitchen appliances. solid oak slats define the floor, and the ceiling is clad in veneered panels.

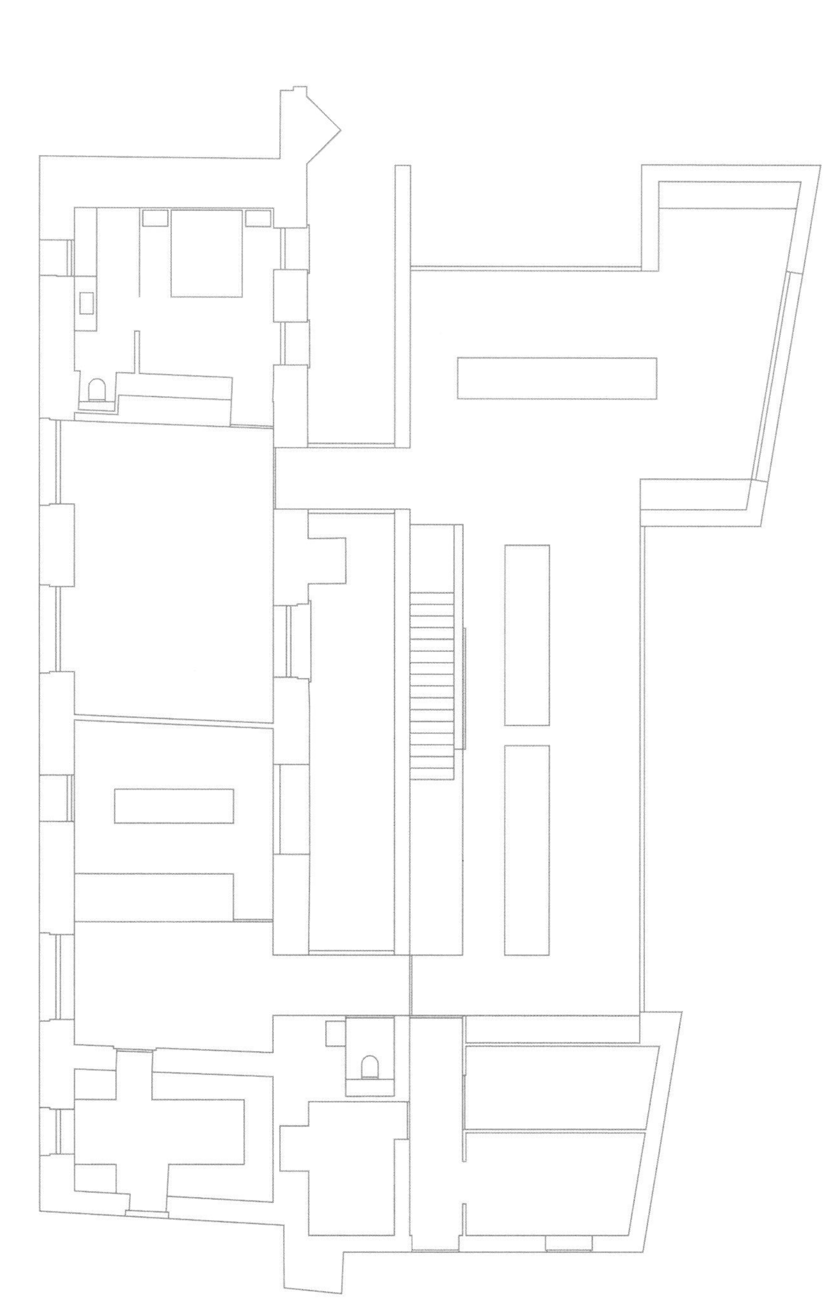

in this project, the emphasis is on tranquillity and expansive views in the living area and bathroom. in both spaces, a concrete floor acts as a sleek, uniform base. the seating area in this muted interior is designed to take full advantage of the views of the garden and pool. the television is discreetly concealed behind a lacquered movable panel next to the fireplace. the compact bathroom, featuring a corian washbasin and bathtub, was extended with an outdoor shower. the subtle handles of the furniture ensure that it blends almost seamlessly into the wall.

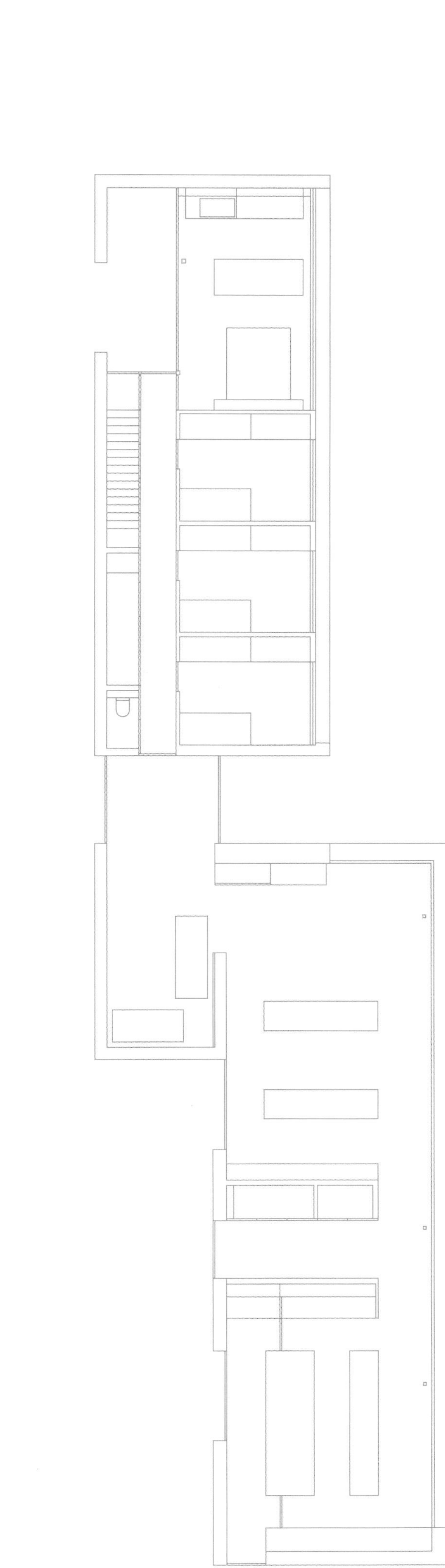

this interior was created for a house designed by govaert & vanhoutte architects. the design starts from the colour palette of the concrete exterior architecture, which is subtly extended inside. weathered oak cabinet walls and a lightly weathered wooden floor create a uniform atmosphere. the doors on either side of the fireplace lead to the master bedroom and the dressing. the grey colour palette is continued in the floor and wall finishes of these spaces, creating a harmonious transition between the different zones.

over the years, we have had the privilege of collaborating with many renowned architects, bringing their plans and visions to life while always preserving the spirit of their design. this often posed considerable technical challenges, which we enjoy. browse a selection of our collaborations on the next pages.

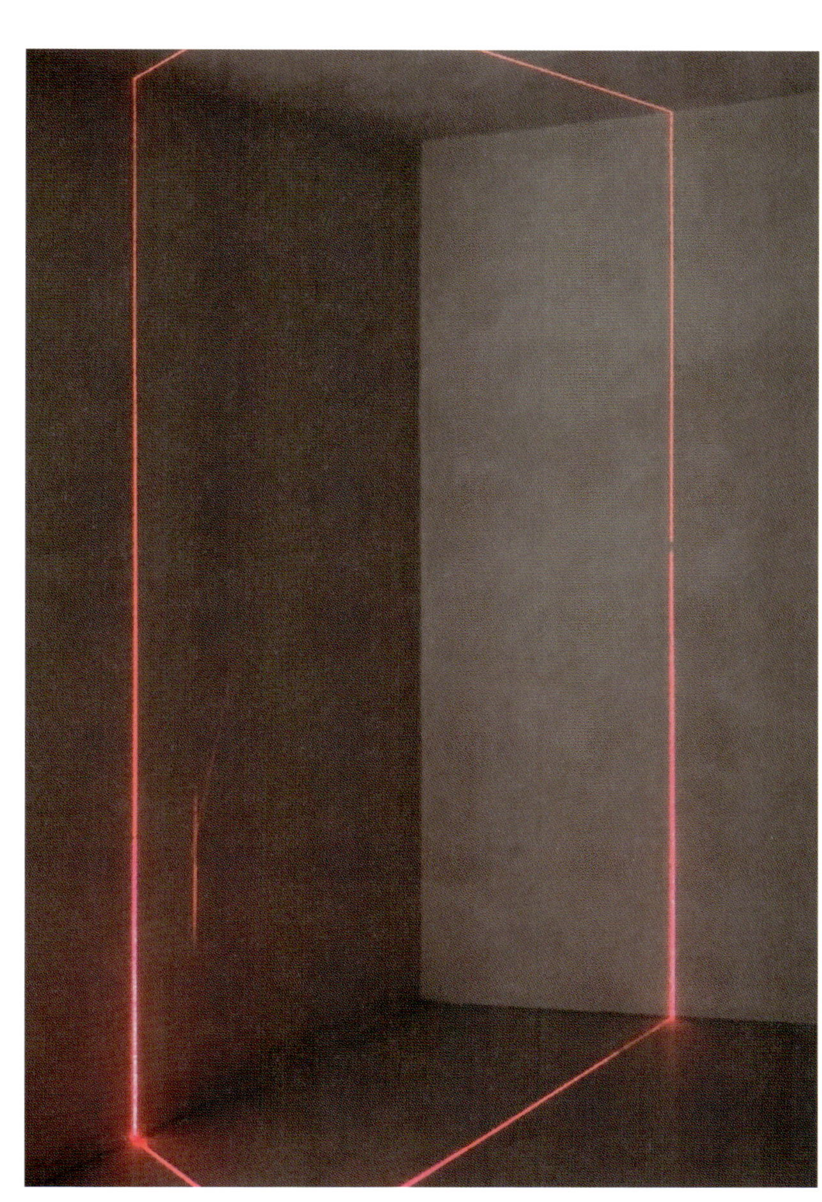

we created a complete interior for this new build. all the living areas are connected and have been positioned in such a way that they offer optimal contact with the stunning surroundings of the marais d'opale. the warm oak parquet contrasts with the darker, loose furniture and the office, which features oak cabinets in deep tones. the kitchen unit is a white volume with an integrated seating area and kitchen appliances that have been discreetly concealed behind doors. a staircase in the entrance hall, which rests on a plinth, leads to the bedrooms on the upper floor.

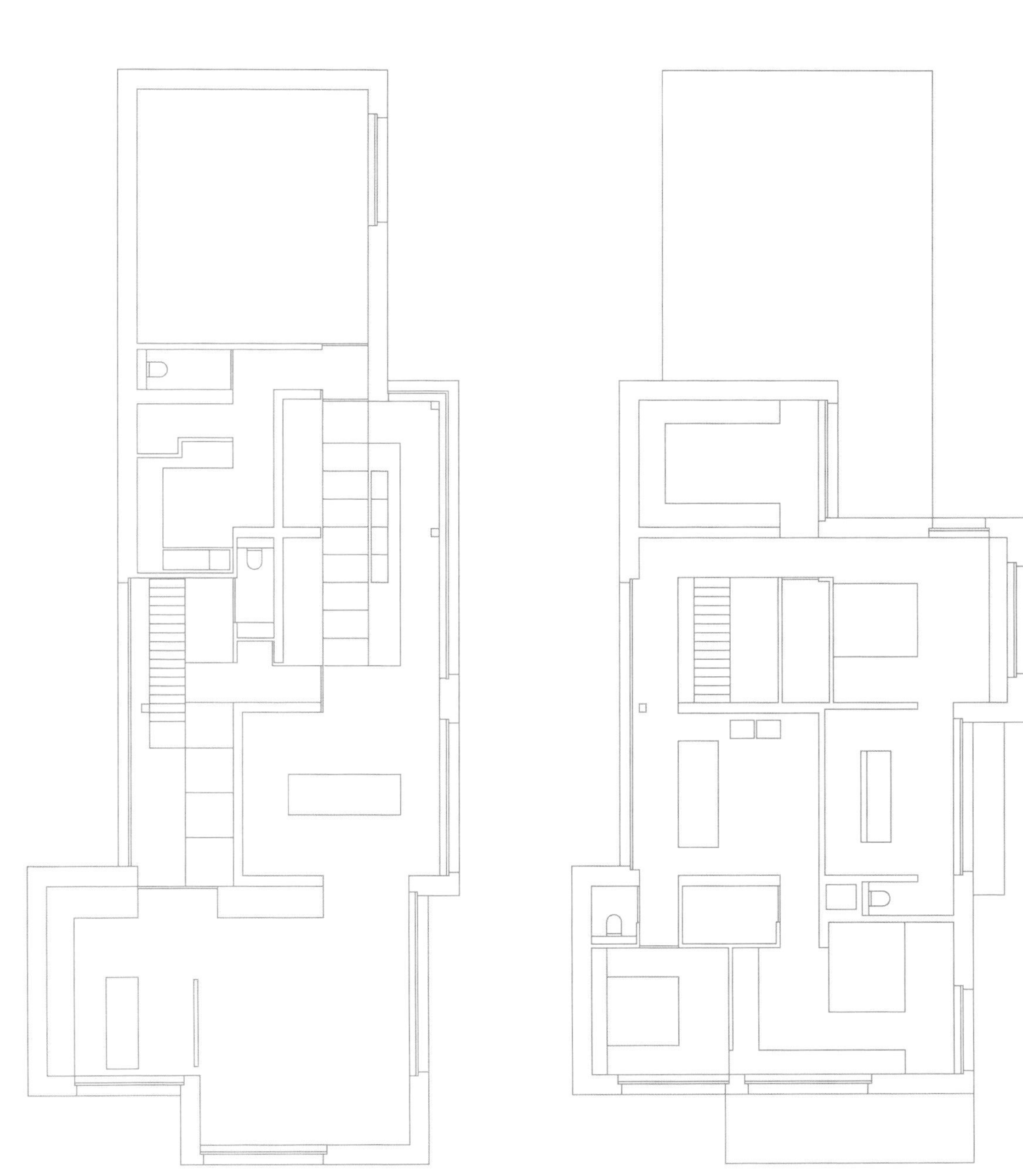

the sleek, bold design of this kitchen, created for a large family that loves to cook, deliberately contrasts with the house's flemish 'fermette' style. the kitchen island anchors the entire interior with its beautiful shades of white and grey. the grey of the carrara marble is repeated in the cast floor, the white in the cabinets. lacquered sliding doors to the side connect the kitchen with the living area and storage room.

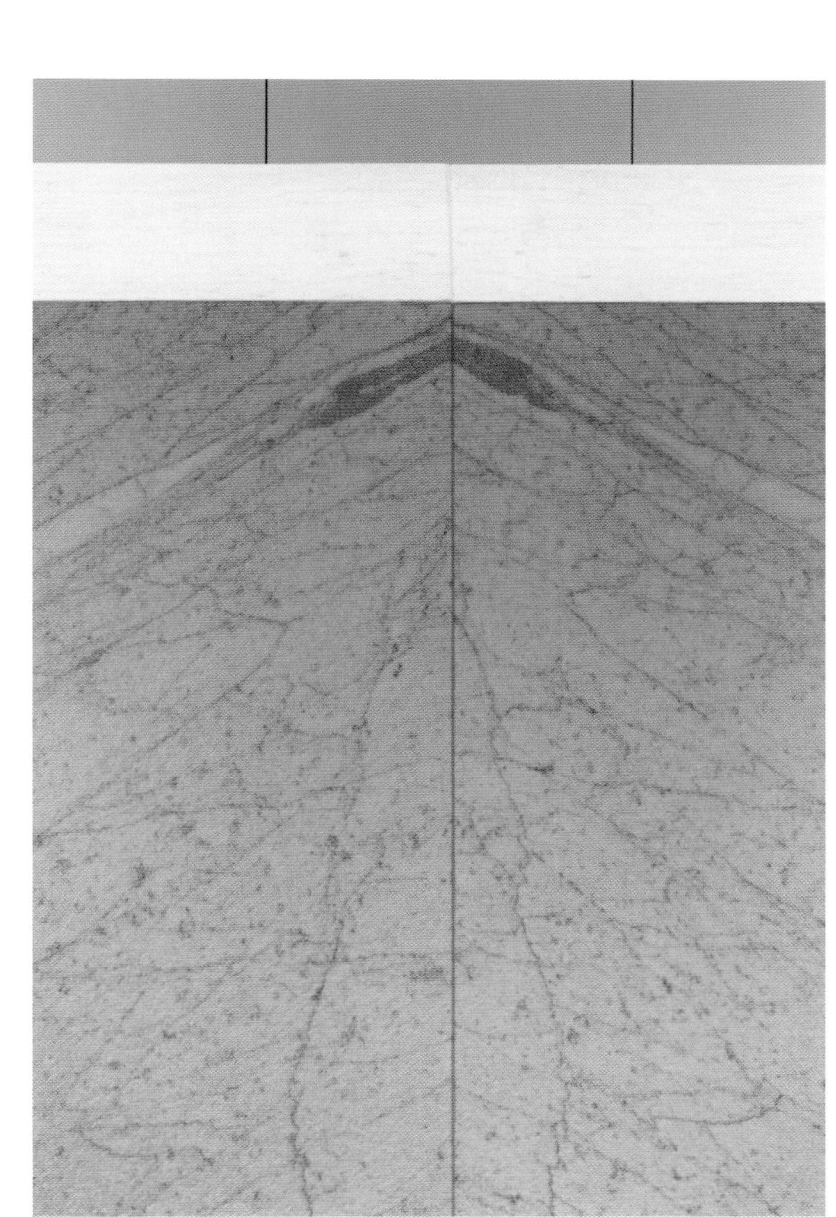

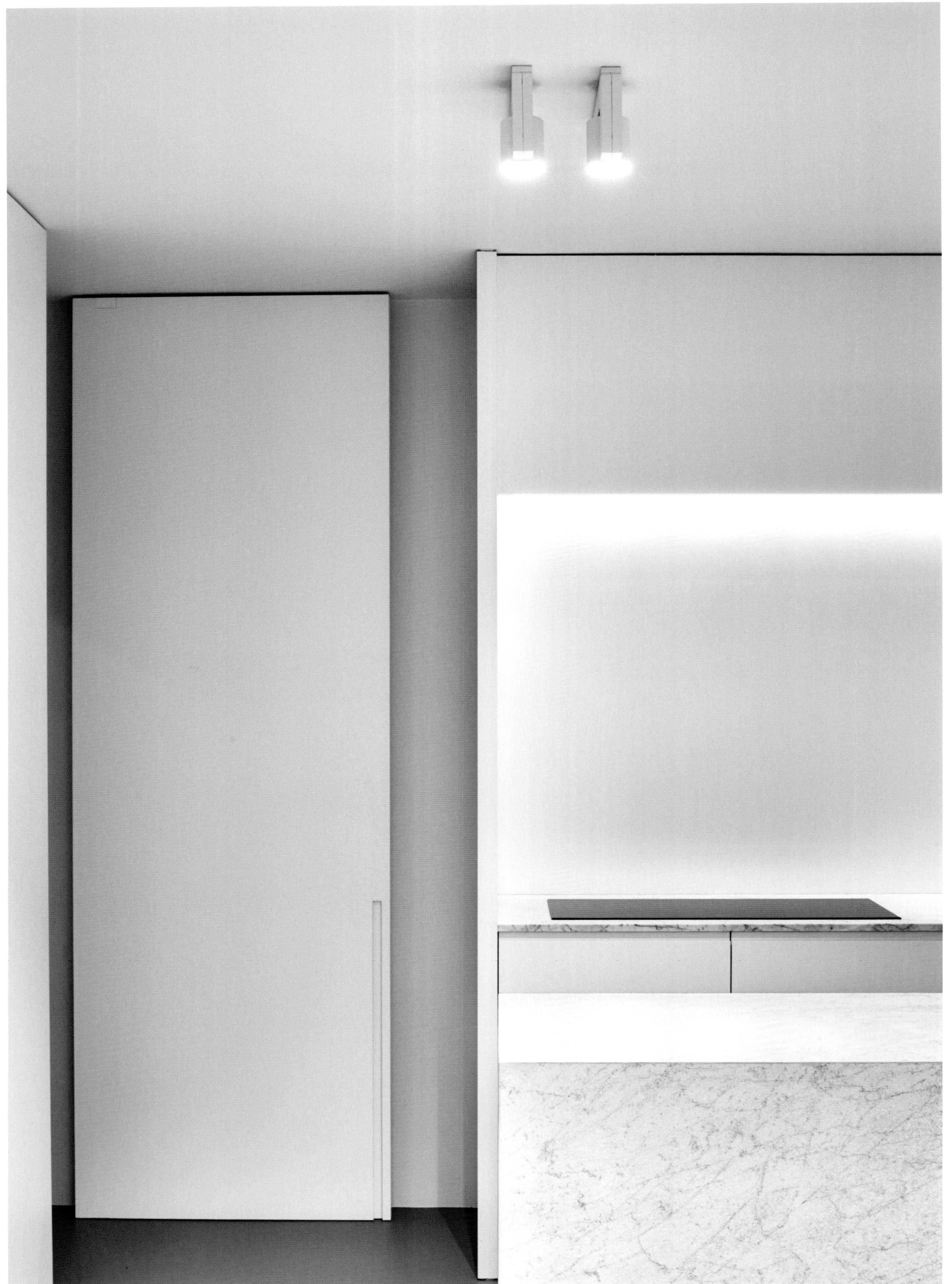

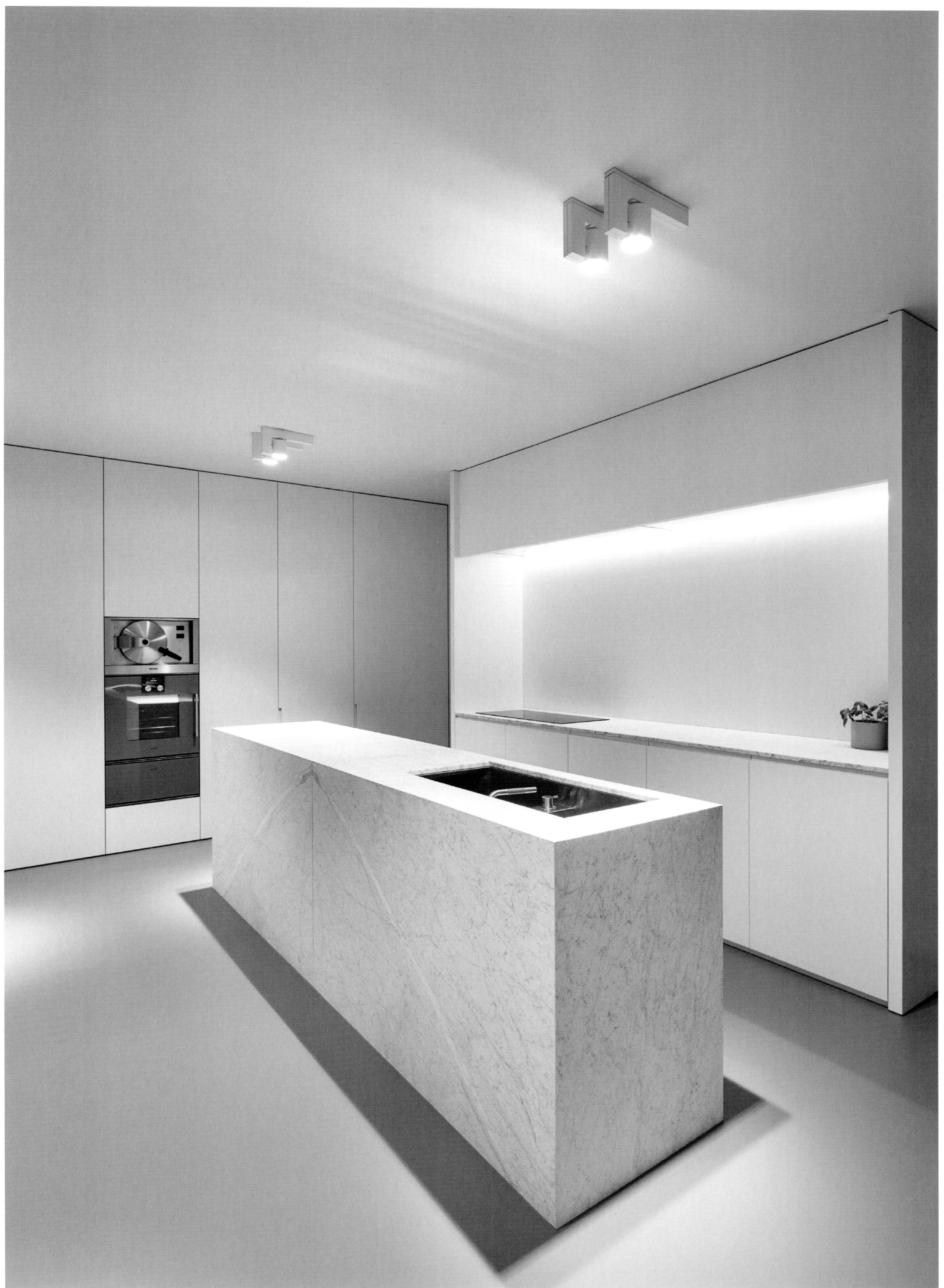

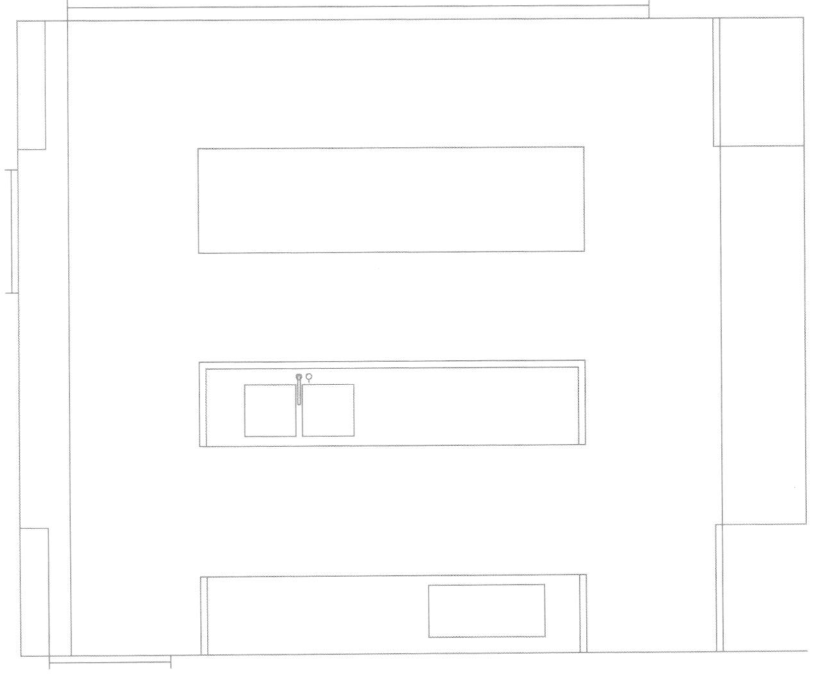

a typical flemish house from the 1980s needed a refresh. whereas the kitchen used to be separate from the living and dining areas, we chose to open everything up, giving the kitchen, which has a garden view, a central place in the house. natural larch added a warm and timeless look and feel. the utility room was also redesigned, with all the functions incorporated in wall cabinets.

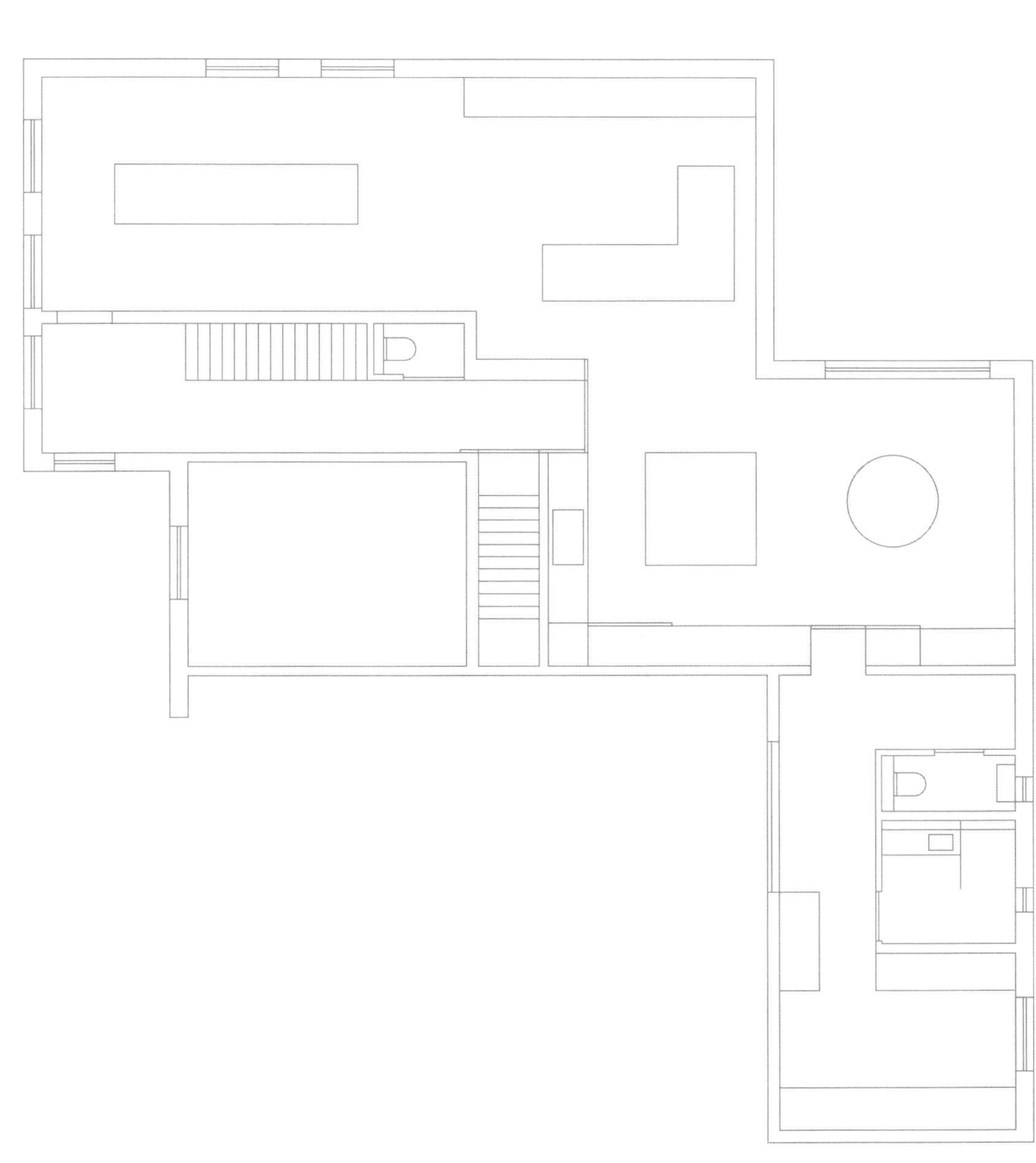

for our own home, we designed furniture and objects that were so popular with our clients that we decided to produce them in small editions. among them are plates for a walking buffet, made from leftovers from our workshop, such as corian and solid wood. other items in our collection include our solid wood table and coffee table. the tabletops appear to hover over the asymmetrical bases, transforming these tables into architectural objects.

the house (from 1920) of wim's great-grandfather was given a major revamp. the original stately front house was retained while the typical flemish 'koterijen' or annexes were demolished to make way for a new volume that is 40 metres deep, 4 metres wide and 4 metres high. the sleeping area is in the historic house, where the existing structure and the original 1920s tiled floor and doors have been preserved as is. the attic has been converted into a mancave. in the new part of the house, floating elements emphasise the length of the volume: the kitchen, fireplace and desk all appear to be suspended from the ceiling, creating a sense of visual space. the distance between the underside of these elements and the floor corresponds with the height of the kitchen island and the dining table. the floors inside and outside are executed in pietra bicci, an italian limestone, which seamlessly matches the colour of the solid wood fronts of all the cabinets.

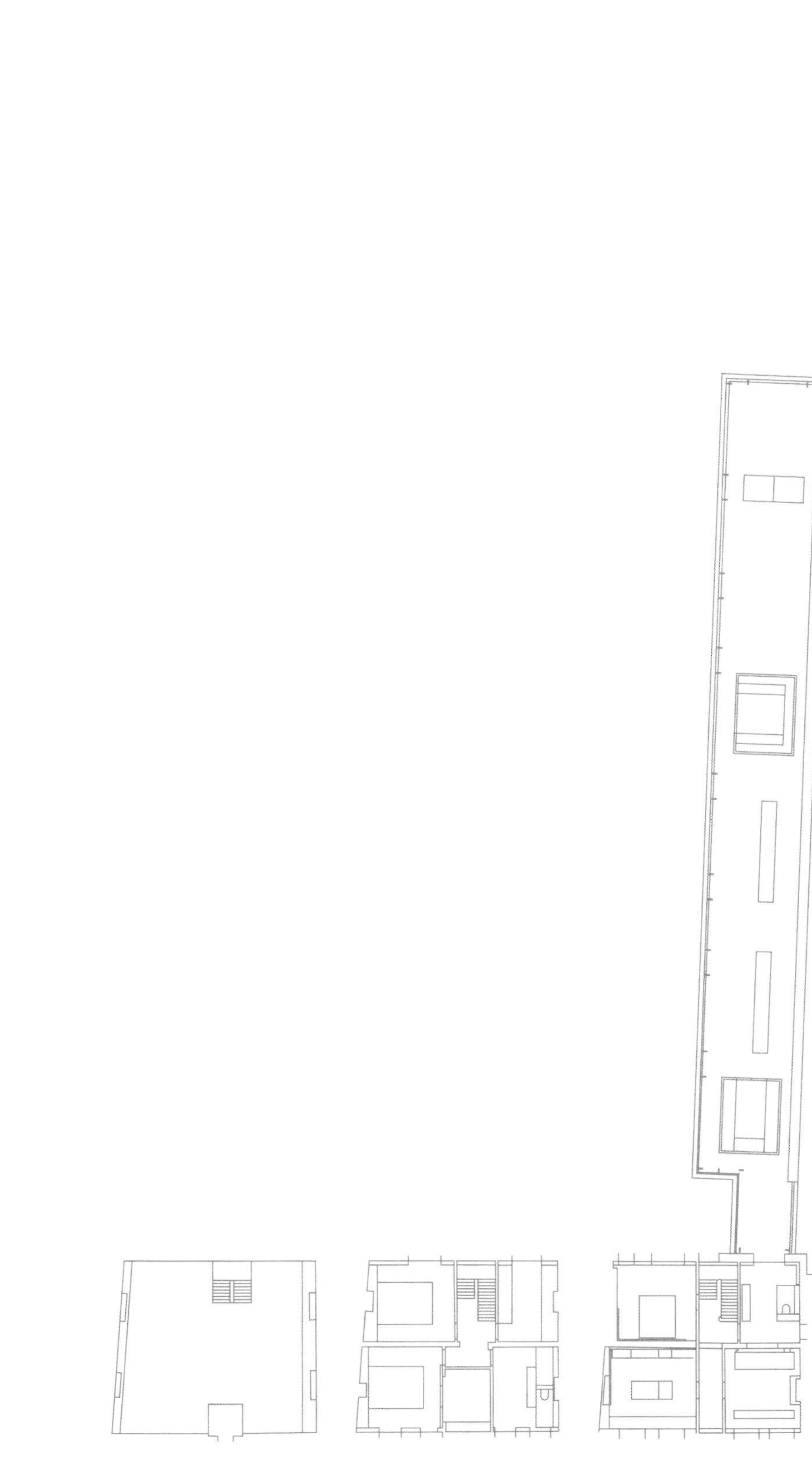

the master suite in this old industrial building was completely opened up to create a large open space. the bathroom consists of two volumes, with one comprising the washbasin and bath. the toilet and shower are concealed behind large mirrored doors.

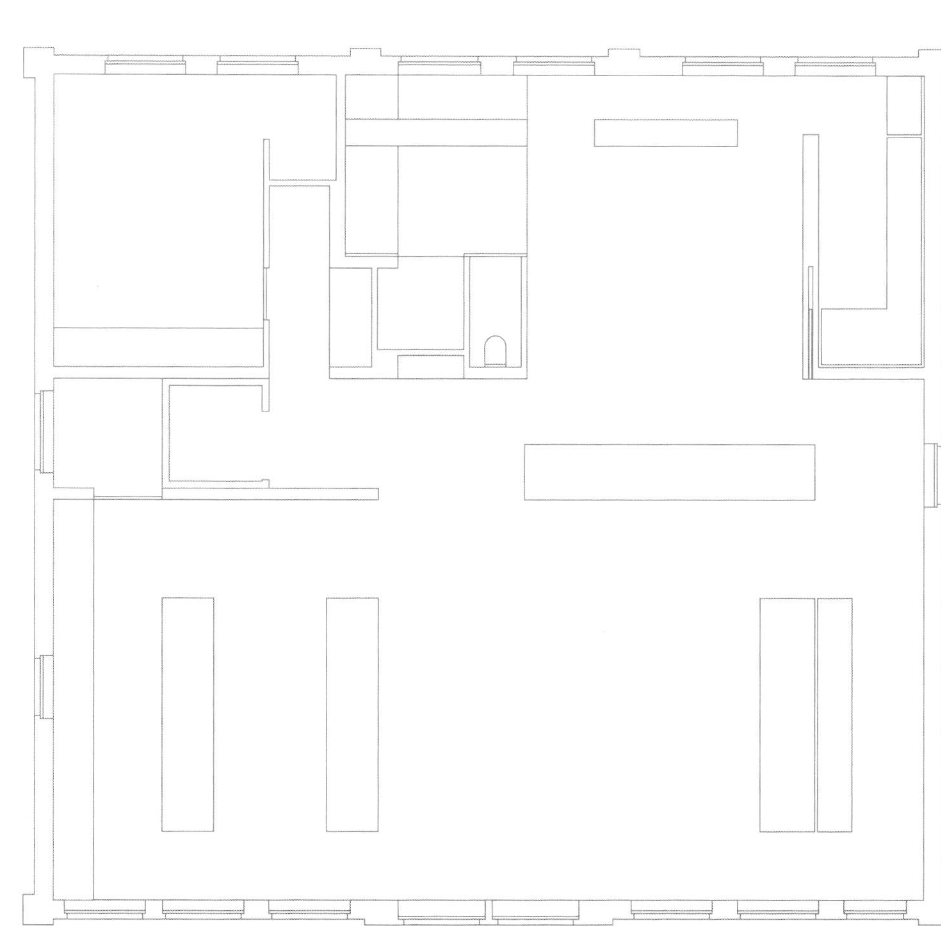

this project comprises two volumes. the living area is housed in a 50-metre-long, elongated volume. the building's length is emphasised even more when the doors are opened. the interior, inspired by a brazilian ambience, features a concrete floor, walnut cabinets, and a kitchen island crafted from ceppo di carnico, an italian limestone. on both sides of the space, glass sliding doors can be fully opened to enhance the indoor-outdoor flow. the second volume, comprising the offices, is housed in a former barn. the original brick wall was preserved, while the solid wood roof slats were repurposed as wall cladding.

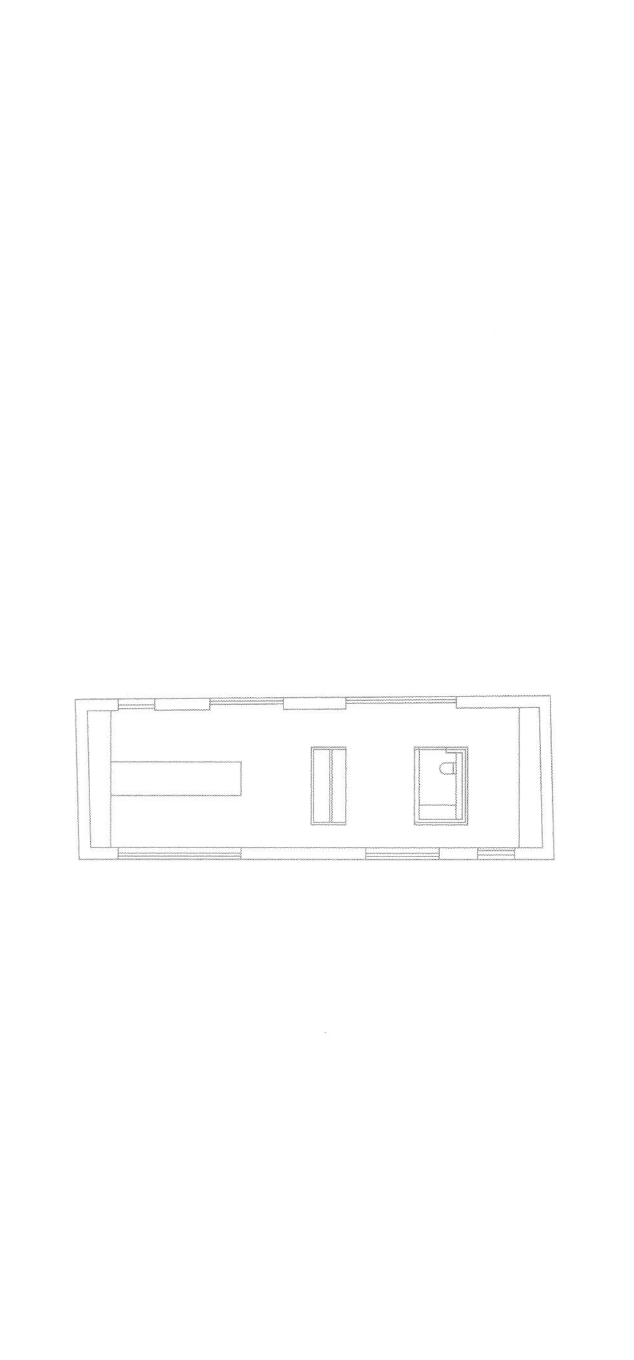

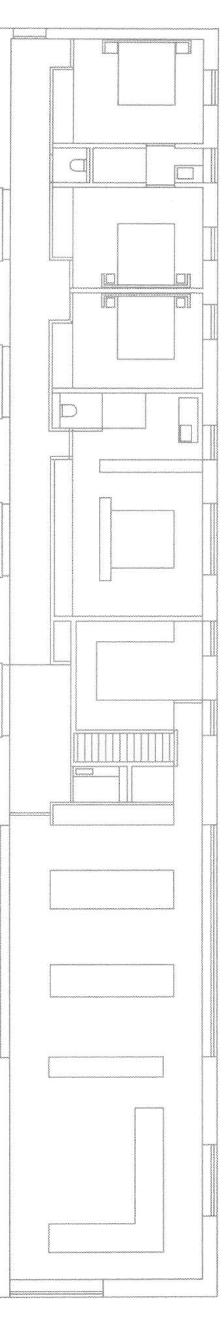

this interior, featuring a kitchen, dining, and sitting area on the upper floor, was designed to take full advantage of the views of the surrounding fields. the horizontal alignment that extends across all the walls adds an eye-catching accent: brushed oak at the bottom in a natural shade, with white cabinet walls above it. the kitchen unit, which is also used as a dining area, is finished in natural stone. the colour of the cast floor in the kitchen and sitting area matches the shades of the wall. there are no distracting elements or eye-catching furniture in the sitting area, ensuring the focus is always on the landscape. the television has been discreetly concealed behind a floating cabinet wall.

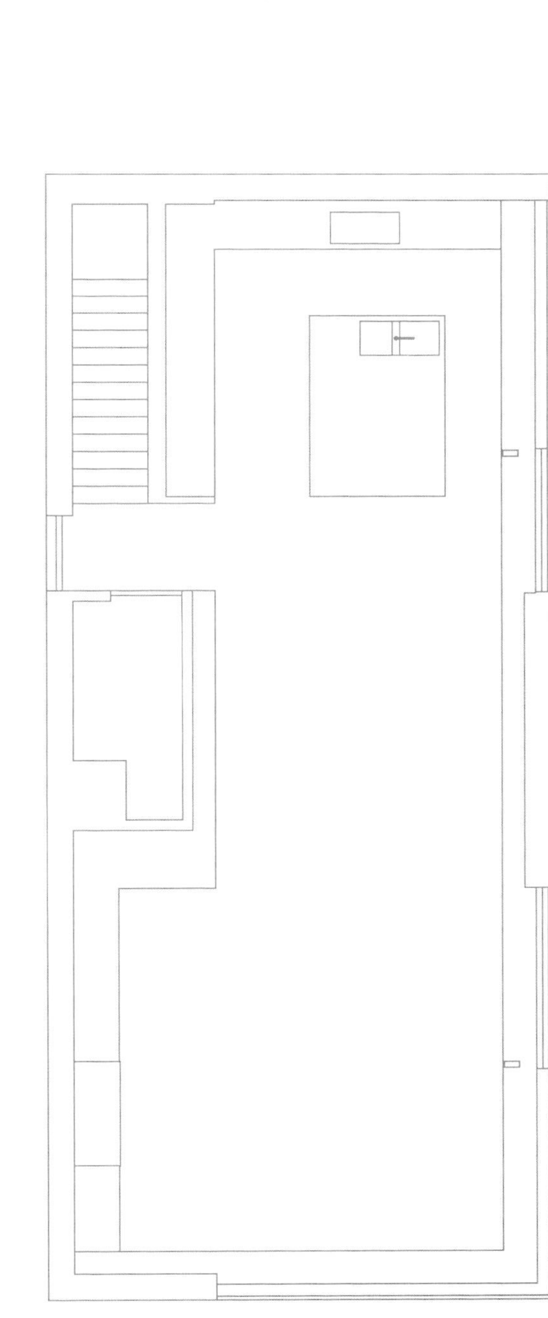

the blue of the scheldt river inspired the choice of blue natural stone for this flat in the nieuw zuid (new south) neighbourhood, paired with walnut wood walls and a dark-toned herringbone parquet. the floor plan was entirely reworked to maximise the flat's floor area, enabling the occupants to fully utilise the space's depth.

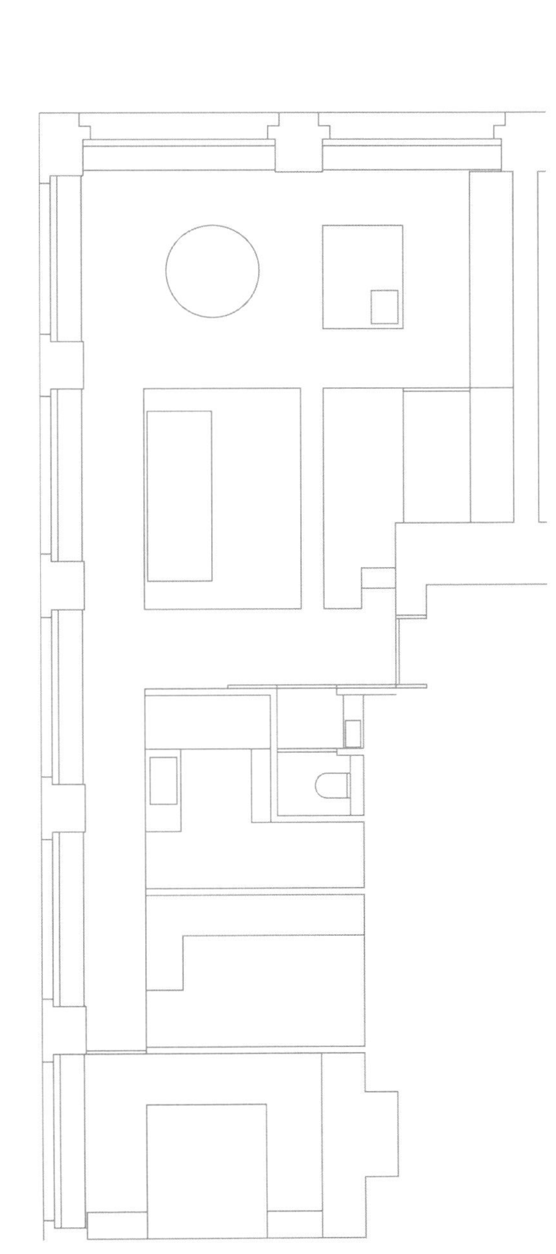

all four floors of this detached listed townhouse in the centre of antwerp were stripped of any disturbing elements that had been added during the many previous renovations as part of its major revamp. all valuable elements were lovingly preserved, and contemporary techniques were fitted to make it a modern home. the kitchen's central volume, in calacatta marble, pairs with the sleek partition walls and cabinet volumes to accentuate the space's grandeur. all the functions of the master suite have been combined in one central volume on the first floor. at the top is a relaxation area, separated from the rest of the house by transparent shutter walls that filter the light and conceal the stairs leading to the roof terrace.

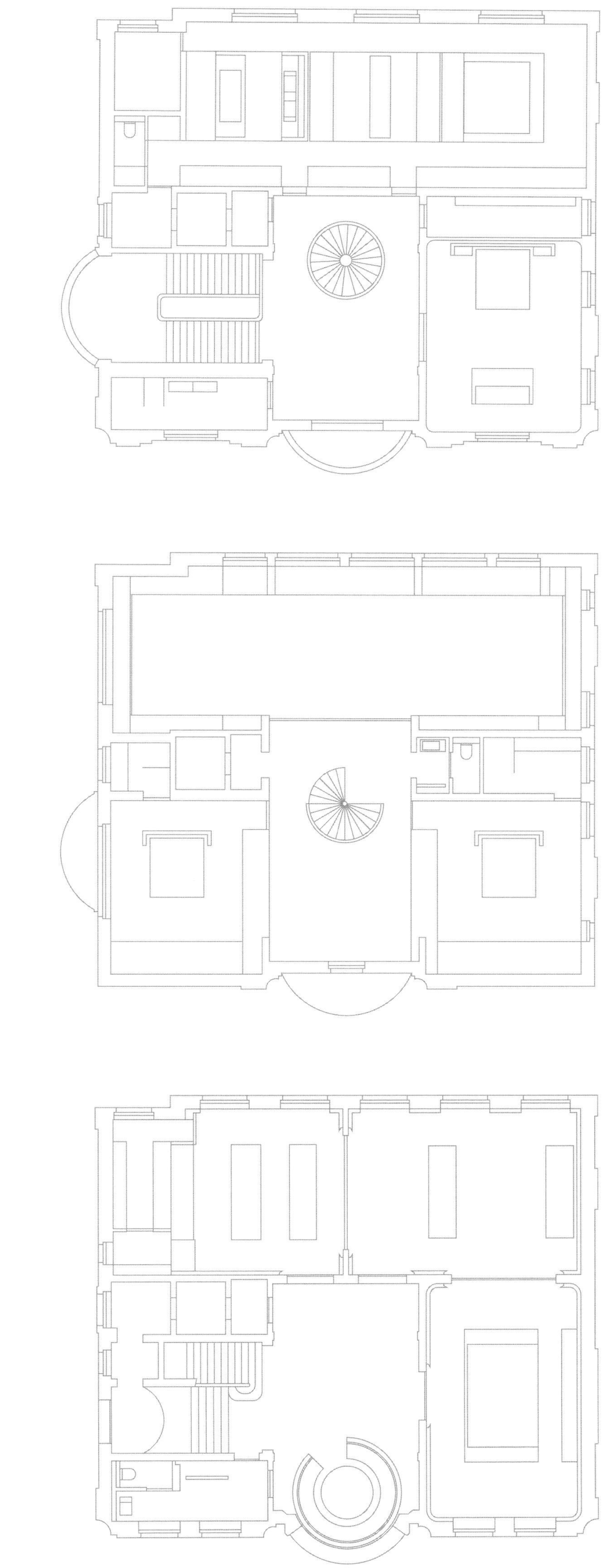

the offices of this door hardware manufacturer needed a timeless look. the rounded green logo served as a guiding principle that recurs in subtle ways throughout the interior. the terrazzo floor and staircase were cast on site. the staircase and reception desk form an architectural whole. everything else is white, in stark contrast with the reception area on the top floor, where the green has been combined with bronze. the rosettes and door handles add a decorative touch.

HDD

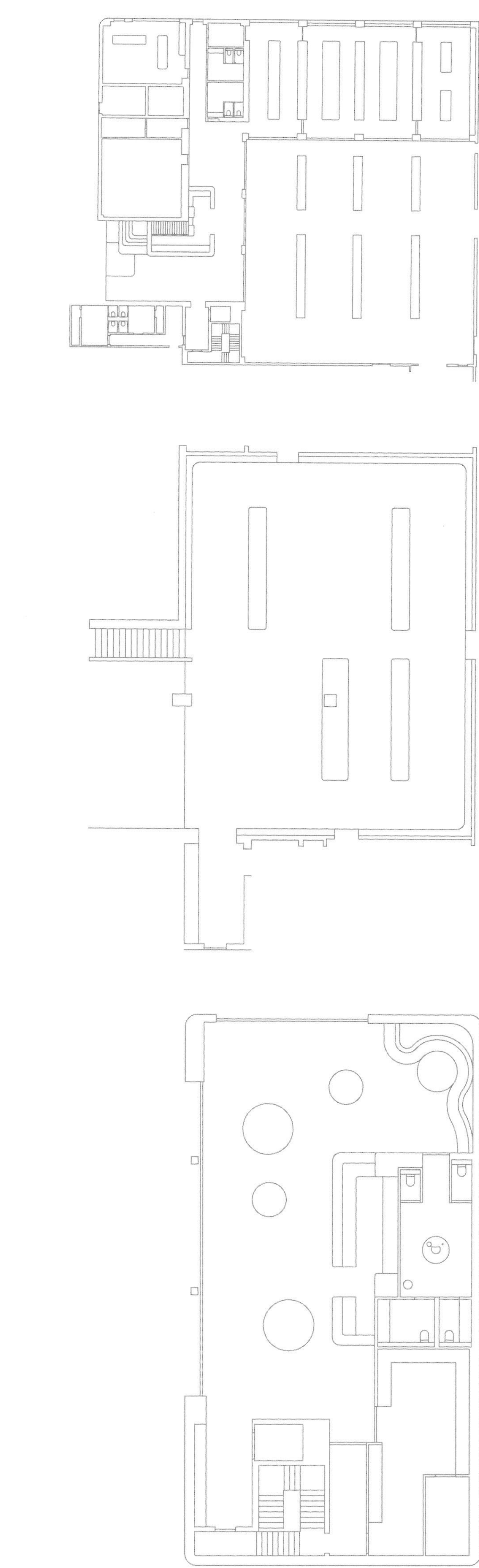

casa lim

in the hills of piedmont, we are currently transforming a typical 1920s dwelling into a minus home, which we will use as a base to visit italian suppliers with our clients. casa lim will also be rented out as a holiday home allowing everyone to immerse themselves in the minus dna. a glimpse of what we have in store…

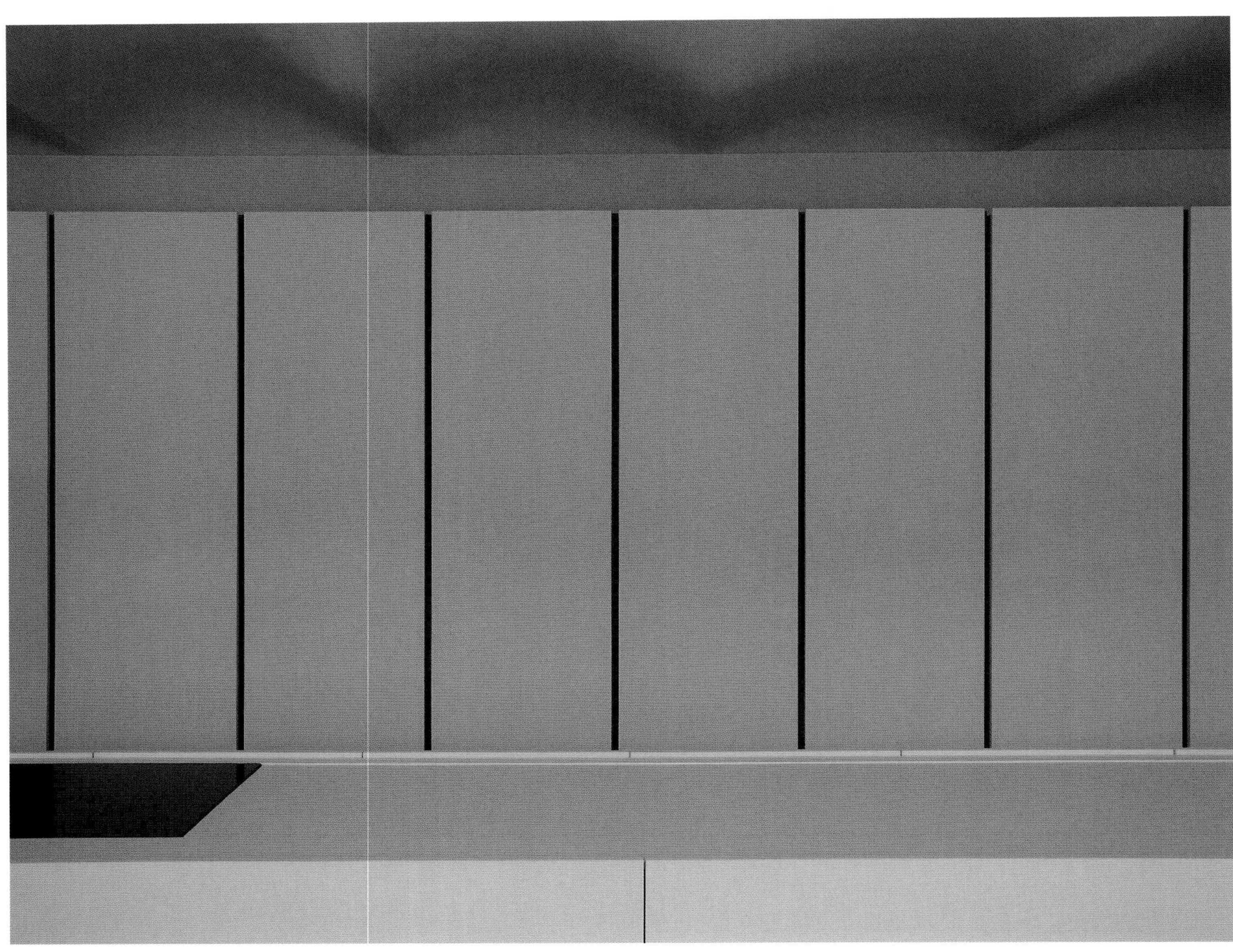

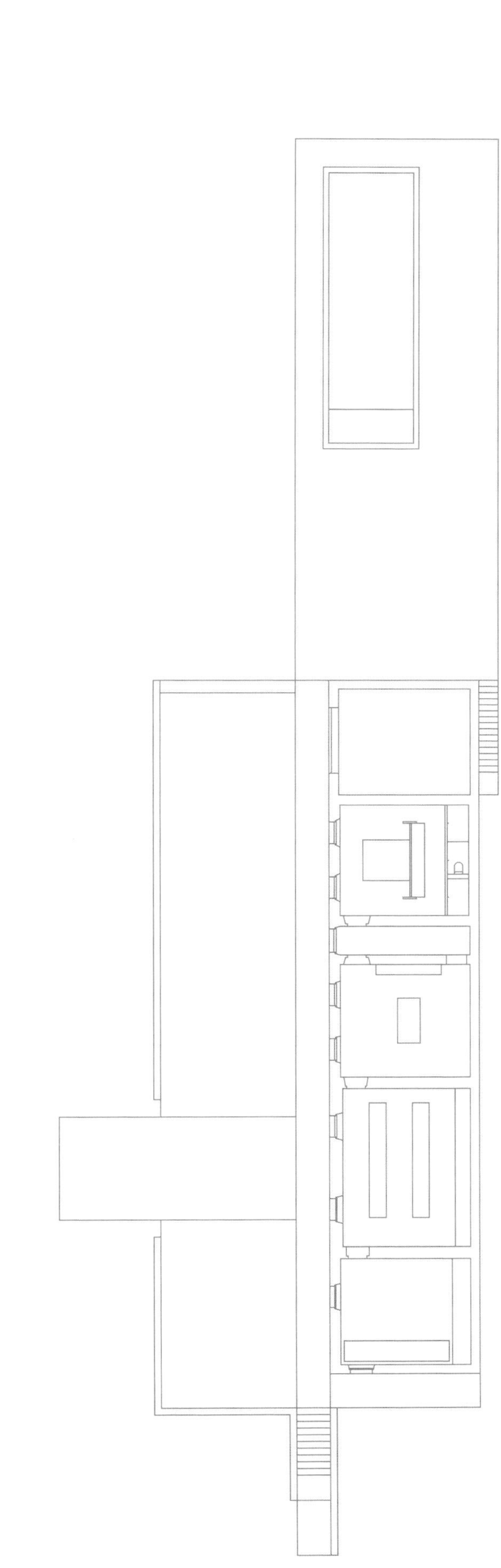

WAGNER

photography

. 00 portraits: alexander popelier
workshop: cafeine
. 01 claude smekens
. 02 claude smekens
. 03 arne jennard
. 04 wim hanenberg
. 05 serge brison
. 06 arne jennard
. 07 arne jennard
. 08 jo pauwels
. 09 cafeine
. 10 cafeine
. 11 cafeine
. 12 cafeine
. 13 collaborations
cafeine
arne jennard
arne jennard
arne jennard
nick cannaerts
arne jennard
wit
. 14 arne jennard
. 15 arne jennard
. 16 arne jennard
. 17 objects: cafeine
. 18 cafeine
. 19 arne jennard
. 20 cafeine
. 21 cafeine, piet albert goethals
. 22 arne jennard
. 23 cafeine
. 24 arne jennard
. 25 minus

colophon

the essence of living

concept, texts, and composition
minus

interview p.5
iris de feijter

final editing and translation
sandy logan

photography
see page opposite

graphic design
bart kiggen

D/2025/12.005/14
isbn 9789460583933
nur 648, 454

info@lusterpublishing.com
lusterpublishing.com
@lusterbooks

printed in italy by printer trento

subscribe to our newsletter for new book alerts and a look behind the scenes: